THEN *God Said,*

"Let There Be

LIGHT"

GENESIS 1:3

THEN

"Let There Be

LIGHT"

GENESIS 1:3

INSPIRING LISTS JOURNAL

DAYMAKER™
An Imprint of Barbour Publishing, Inc.

Published by DayMaker, an imprint of Barbour Publishing, Inc., P.O. Box 719, Uhrichsville, Ohio 44683, www.barbourbooks.com

Our mission is to publish and distribute inspirational products offering exceptional value and biblical encouragement to the masses.

 Member of the
Evangelical Christian
Publishers Association

Printed in the United States of America.

MY
"Favorite Memories"
LIST

_____
_____
_____
_____
_____
_____
_____
_____
_____
_____
_____
_____
_____
_____
_____
_____
_____
_____
_____
_____
_____
_____
_____
_____
_____

MY
"Plans I Believe God Has for Me"
LIST

MY
"Ways I'd Like to Change the World"
LIST

MY
"Most Amazing Qualities and Talents"
LIST

MY
"Favorite Bible People"
LIST

_____
_____
_____
_____
_____
_____
_____
_____
_____
_____
_____
_____
_____
_____
_____
_____
_____
_____
_____
_____
_____
_____
_____
_____
_____

MY
"Phobias and Fears"
LIST

_____
_____
_____
_____
_____
_____
_____
_____
_____
_____
_____
_____
_____
_____
_____
_____
_____
_____
_____
_____
_____
_____
_____
_____
_____

MY
"Most Courageous Moments"
LIST

MY
"Things Most People Don't Know About Me (but God Does)"
LIST

MY
"praying For. . ."
LIST

MY
"Favorite People I Like to Have Around Me"
LIST

MY
"Most Thankful For. . ."
LIST

_____
_____
_____
_____
_____
_____
_____
_____
_____
_____
_____
_____
_____
_____
_____
_____
_____
_____
_____
_____
_____
_____

MY
"Reasons I Love My Life"
LIST

MY
"Favorite Words of All Time"
LIST

MY
"Favorite Bible Verses"
LIST

MY
"I Wish Some Things Were Different"
LIST

MY
"Hopes and Dreams"
LIST

MY
"Thoughts About God"
LIST

MY
"Life in Single Words"
LIST

MY
"Favorite Critters Created by God"
LIST

MY
"Wish I Had a Do-Over"
LIST

MY
"Thoughts on Heaven"
LIST

MY
"I Am Blessed"
LIST

MY
"Life Lessons Learned from Afar"
LIST

MY
"Biggest Questions About Life"
LIST

MY
"Favorite Foods of All Time"
LIST

MY
"Things I'd Take with Me to a Deserted Island"
LIST

MY
"Essentials to a Happy Life"
LIST

MY
"People Who Have Had the Greatest Impact on My Life"
LIST

MY
"Habits I'd Like to Break"
LIST

MY
"Favorite Songs"
LIST

MY
"Favorite Places I've Visited"
LIST

MY
"Want to Go There in My Lifetime"
LIST

MY
"Meh, Could Live with It or without It"
LIST

MY
"Favorite Books I've Read"
LIST

MY
"Favorite Promises from God's Word"
LIST

MY
"Can't Live without It"
LIST

MY
"Most Embarrassing Moments of All Time"
LIST

MY
"Wisest Decisions of All Time"
LIST

MY
"Dumbest Decisions of All Time"
LIST

MY
"Lifelong Friends"
LIST

MY
"Most Adventurous Moments"
LIST

MY
"I Wonder Why They Did That?"
LIST

MY
"People I Miss the Most"
LIST

MY
"Favorite Stories of the Bible"
LIST

MY
"Ways I Like to Share My Faith"
LIST

MY
"Fashion Don'ts"
LIST

MY
"Things That Make Me Nervous"
LIST

MY
"Favorite Jokes"
LIST

_____

_____

_____

_____

_____

_____

_____

_____

_____

_____

_____

_____

_____

_____

_____

_____

_____

_____

_____

_____

_____

MY
"Ways I Like to Spread Joy"
LIST

MY
"I Know It's Ridiculous, But. . ."
LIST

MY
"God Makes Miracles Happen"
LIST

MY
"God Answers Prayer"
LIST

MY
"Needs Improvement"
LIST

MY
"World Issues I Care Most About"
LIST

_____
_____
_____
_____
_____
_____
_____
_____
_____
_____
_____
_____
_____
_____
_____
_____
_____
_____
_____
_____
_____
_____
_____

MY
"Community Issues I Care Most About"
LIST

MY
"What I Love Best About My Family"
LIST

_____

_____

_____

_____

_____

_____

_____

_____

_____

_____

_____

_____

_____

_____

_____

_____

_____

_____

_____

_____

_____

_____

_____

MY
"Biggest Worries"
LIST

MY
"I Know God's Got This"
LIST

MY
"Favorite Things to Do with Friends"
LIST

_____

_____

_____

_____

_____

_____

_____

_____

_____

_____

_____

_____

_____

_____

_____

_____

_____

_____

_____

_____

_____

_____

_____

MY
"I'm So Glad God Said Yes. . ."
LIST

_____

_____

_____

_____

_____

_____

_____

_____

_____

_____

_____

_____

_____

_____

_____

_____

_____

_____

_____

_____

_____

_____

_____

_____

_____

_____

_____

_____

MY
"It's a Good Thing God Said No"
LIST

_____
_____
_____
_____
_____
_____
_____
_____
_____
_____
_____
_____
_____
_____
_____
_____
_____
_____
_____
_____
_____
_____
_____
_____
_____

MY
"God Is Making Me Wait"
LIST

MY
"Things I Need to Forgive"
LIST

MY
"Reasons I Have Hope"
LIST

MY
"Favorite Things About My Church"
LIST

MY
"Need to Make Some Changes"
LIST

MY
"Biggest Heartbreaks and Disappointments"
LIST

MY
"Ways I Serve"
LIST

MY
"Ways I Share God's Love"
LIST

MY
"Dream Careers"
LIST

MY
"Life Is Too Short, So. . ."
LIST

MY
"Best Advice I've Ever Received"
LIST

_____
_____
_____
_____
_____
_____
_____
_____
_____
_____
_____
_____
_____
_____
_____
_____
_____
_____
_____
_____
_____
_____
_____
_____
_____

MY
"Best Advice I've Ever Given"
LIST

MY
"I Wish I Would Have. . ."
LIST

MY
"Hard Lessons Learned in Life"
LIST

MY
"Without God, My Life Was. . ."
LIST

MY
"With God, My Life Is. . ."
LIST

_____

_____

_____

_____

_____

_____

_____

_____

_____

_____

_____

_____

_____

_____

_____

_____

_____

_____

_____

_____

_____

_____

_____

_____

_____

_____

MY
"Moments I've Surprised Myself"
LIST

MY
"Too Good Not to Share"
LIST

MY
"Moments When God Got My Attention"
LIST

MY
"Favorite Ways to Spend Free Time"
LIST

MY
"Ways My Faith Has Influenced My Decisions"
LIST

MY
"Strange but True Things About Me"
LIST

MY
"Thoughts on God's Word"
LIST

MY
"I Am a Work in Progress"
LIST

MY
"I Didn't Know I Had the Strength"
LIST

MY
"Things That Build My Confidence"
LIST

MY
"Life's Biggest Challenges"
LIST

MY
"Favorite Jobs of All Time"
LIST

_____

_____

_____

_____

_____

_____

_____

_____

_____

_____

_____

_____

_____

_____

_____

_____

_____

_____

_____

_____

_____

MY
"Worst Jobs of All Time"
LIST

MY
"Wise Money Management"
LIST

MY
"Words That Lift My Spirit"
LIST

_____
_____
_____
_____
_____
_____
_____
_____
_____
_____
_____
_____
_____
_____
_____
_____
_____
_____
_____
_____
_____
_____
_____
_____
_____

MY
"Ways I Like to Relax"
LIST

MY
"Putting Others First"
LIST

MY
"Necessities for a Victorious Life"
LIST

MY
"Faith Is a Part of My Everyday Life"
LIST

_____
_____
_____
_____
_____
_____
_____
_____
_____
_____
_____
_____
_____
_____
_____
_____
_____
_____
_____
_____
_____

MY
"Things That Bring Me Comfort"
LIST

MY
"Experiences That Have Increased My Faith"
LIST

MY
"Prayer Changes Things"
LIST

MY
"God Cares About the Small Stuff"
LIST

MY
"God Cares About the Big Stuff"
LIST

MY
"Keep It Simple"
LIST

MY
"Biggest Encouragers"
LIST

MY
"When Life Throws You Lemons. . . Tips"
LIST

MY
"Ways God Has Shown Me Favor in Life"
LIST

MY
"Moments I've Wanted to Give Up"
LIST

MY
"Moments I'm So Glad I Didn't Give Up"
LIST

MY
"Random Thoughts"
LIST

MY
"Reasons I Trust God"
LIST

_____
_____
_____
_____
_____
_____
_____
_____
_____
_____
_____
_____
_____
_____
_____
_____
_____
_____
_____
_____
_____

MY
"Least Favorite Words"
LIST

MY
"I Wish I Had Invented That"
LIST

MY
"Life's Lightbulb Moments"
LIST

_____
_____
_____
_____
_____
_____
_____
_____
_____
_____
_____
_____
_____
_____
_____
_____
_____
_____
_____
_____
_____
_____
_____
_____
_____

MY
"Favorite People in History"
LIST

MY
"Advice I'd Give the President"
LIST

MY
"When _____, I Know It's Going to Be a Great Day"
LIST

MY
"When _____, I Know a Bad Day Is Looming" LIST

MY
"Things That Give Me the Creeps"
LIST

MY
"Things That Make Me Smile"
LIST

MY
"I Wonder Why"
LIST

MY
"Someday"
LIST

MY
"I Wonder How They Did That?"
LIST

MY
"Favorite Books of the Bible"
LIST

MY
"Things I'd Rather Not Share (but Know I Should)"
LIST

_____
_____
_____
_____
_____
_____
_____
_____
_____
_____
_____
_____
_____
_____
_____
_____
_____
_____
_____
_____
_____
_____
_____
_____
_____

MY
"Reasons I Should Show Love to Everyone I Meet"
LIST

MY
*"It's Really Not **That** Important"*
LIST

MY
"Words That Describe My Faith"
LIST

MY
"Favorite Pets from My Past"
LIST

MY
"Favorite Indoor Activities"
LIST

_____
_____
_____
_____
_____
_____
_____
_____
_____
_____
_____
_____
_____
_____
_____
_____
_____
_____
_____
_____
_____
_____
_____

MY
"Favorite Outdoor Activities"
LIST

MY
"Random What-If"
LIST

MY
"Bizarre Words and Phrases"
LIST

MY
"Things That Make Me Cry"
LIST

MY
"Things I Can't Stand"
LIST

MY
"Words That Best Describe Me"
LIST

MY
"What God's Word Has Taught Me About Life"
LIST

MY
"What Prayer Has Taught Me About Life"
LIST

MY
"When I Think About God. . ."
LIST

MY
"Hard Things I'm Thankful to Have Experienced"
LIST

MY
"People I Thank God for Every Day"
LIST

MY
"Why Didn't I Think of That?"
LIST

MY
"Questions I'd Like to Ask God"
LIST

MY
"Things I've Wondered About but Never Bothered to Research"
LIST

_____

_____

_____

_____

_____

_____

_____

_____

_____

_____

_____

_____

_____

_____

_____

_____

_____

_____

_____

_____

_____

_____

MY
"Strange Foods I've Tasted"
LIST

MY
"Bucket"
LIST

_____
_____
_____
_____
_____
_____
_____
_____
_____
_____
_____
_____
_____
_____
_____
_____
_____
_____
_____
_____
_____
_____
_____
_____
_____

MY
"Things I'm Most Passionate About"
LIST

_____
_____
_____
_____
_____
_____
_____
_____
_____
_____
_____
_____
_____
_____
_____
_____
_____
_____
_____
_____
_____
_____
_____
_____
_____

MY
"Words I Use but Don't Know What They Actually Mean"
LIST

MY
"Experiences That Have Made Me a Better Person"
LIST

MY
"Hobbies"
LIST

MY
"Chores I Despise"
LIST

MY
"Celebrities I'd Like to Hang Out with for a Day"
LIST

MY
"Things I'd Like God to Change"
LIST

MY
"How I Think Others Would Describe Me"
LIST

MY
"Things I Need to Give to God"
LIST

_____
_____
_____
_____
_____
_____
_____
_____
_____
_____
_____
_____
_____
_____
_____
_____
_____
_____
_____
_____
_____

MY
"Thumbs Up"
LIST

MY
"Thumbs Down"
LIST

MY
"Words That Describe My Best Friends"
LIST

MY
"Words That Describe My Family"
LIST

MY
"People I'd Like to Hug"
LIST

MY
"Family Traditions"
LIST

MY
"Ways I Like to Be Creative"
LIST

MY
"Things I've Lost but Never Found"
LIST

MY
"If I Could Do Anything I Wanted Today, It Would Be. . ."
LIST

MY
"I Wish It Were as Good for Me as It Tastes"
LIST

MY
"Someone Should Invent. . ."
LIST

MY
"Things That Make Me Say 'Aww!'"
LIST

MY
"Songs That Make Me Wish I Could Breakdance"
LIST

MY
"I Can't Believe I Really Said That"
LIST

MY
"God Is So Good"
LIST

MY
"Just Once, I'd Like To. . ."
LIST

_____

_____

_____

_____

_____

_____

_____

_____

_____

_____

_____

_____

_____

_____

_____

_____

_____

_____

_____

_____

_____

MY
"Things I'd Never Do Again If I Didn't Have To"
LIST

MY
"Things I Never Get Sick Of"
LIST

MY
"Ways I'd Like to Be Remembered"
LIST